Bernard of Hollywood's

Marilyn

Text and Edited by
SUSAN BERNARD

ST. MARTIN'S PRESS
New York

In memory of my mother,
Ruth Brande Bernard,
and my dad, Bruno Bernard,
whose loving presences prevail.

Many people and friends have contributed to making this book possible: Jim Fitzgerald, my genius of an editor who understands the osmosis between two artists; Bob Tabian, my dedicated and innovative agent—I am forever grateful to them for bringing the grand vision behind this book to fruition—Deborah Daly, the designer, for being sensitive enough to work along with my suggestions while implementing her artistic insights; Karen Gillis, director of manufacturing at St. Martin's Press, for putting the collection on the pedestal where it belongs.

For their help in continuing to publish and preserve the integrity of Dad's work with Marilyn, and those who have given in the past and present assistance and inspiration which is the foundation of this book, I want to thank, in alphabetical order: The Academy of Motion Picture Arts and Sciences for honoring dad, Russell Adams, All About Marilyn, Lisa Bankoff, Jed Bark, Celeste Bendelle, Jay Bernstein, Dr. Leon and Mildred Boxer, Dr. Michael Boxer, Norman Brokaw, Mario Cassili, Sylvia Cohen, Steve and Sheryl Conway, Joseph and Patricia Cotten, Vince Dajiri, Yvonne De Carlo, Nick Dubrule, Doug Edwards, Angelina Emanuelle, Andy Ettinger, Madeleine Fishman, Clark Gable, Julie Galant, Philippe Halsman, Sandra Harmon, G. Ray Hawkins, Hugh Hefner, Axel Hubert, Bill Inoshita, Ruile James, Dr. Nancy Johnson, Theron Kabrich, Diane Keaton, Kensal Press, Sid Klevatt, Debbie Koehnlein, Linda Krikorian, Alex Kuczynski, David Ladd, Larry Lawrence, Ken and Julie Levtow, George and Maria Lombard, Margaret Herrick Library, Linda Mehr, Tony Merkin, Deborah Miller, Jason Miller, Keith Miller, Earl Mills, Susan Muchnic, Munich Film Festival, James Munro, Don Murray, Lu Murray, Anaïs Nin, Palm Springs International Film Festival, Palm Springs Racquet Club, Patricia Poppili, Paul Pospesil, Richard Raab, Jeanne Rejaunier, Sonya Retilley, Alan Rich, Roger Richman, Susan Robinson, Ginger Rogers, Dr. Richard Rosenthal, Dick Rosenzweig, Diane Sawyer, Ron Schick, Lothar Schirmer, George Shdanoff, Alyssa Sherwood, Pat Shields, Maria Shriver, Lili St. Cyr, Edwige St. Jacques, Sol and Adele Tannenbaum, Hendrik te Neues, Kevin Thomas, Alberto Vargas, Princess Irene von Anhalt, Dr. Donald and Sharon Wallens, Bruce Weber, Walter Winchell, and a special thanks to Richard Thalheimer whose brilliance launched Dad's Norma Jean across four continents, his Sharper Image staff, and to the millions of faithful collectors and fans.

I am especially grateful to: Rod Vulich, my creative and relentless marketing director; Coro Chase, my assistant since the birth of Bernard of Hollywood publishing, who has served with wisdom and excellence; Arthur Stashower, my longtime friend and legal guardian angel; my dearest friend, photojournalist Marianna Diamos, for everlasting moral support.

I owe a very special thanks to my talented and remarkable son, Joshua Miller, for enduring overwhelming pain and joy since Marilyn became a member of our family, and for his encouragement and participation in honoring his grandfather's legacy.

Design by Deborah Daly

ISBN 0-312-08882-5

First Edition: April 1993
10 9 8 7 6 5 4 3 2 1

CONTENTS

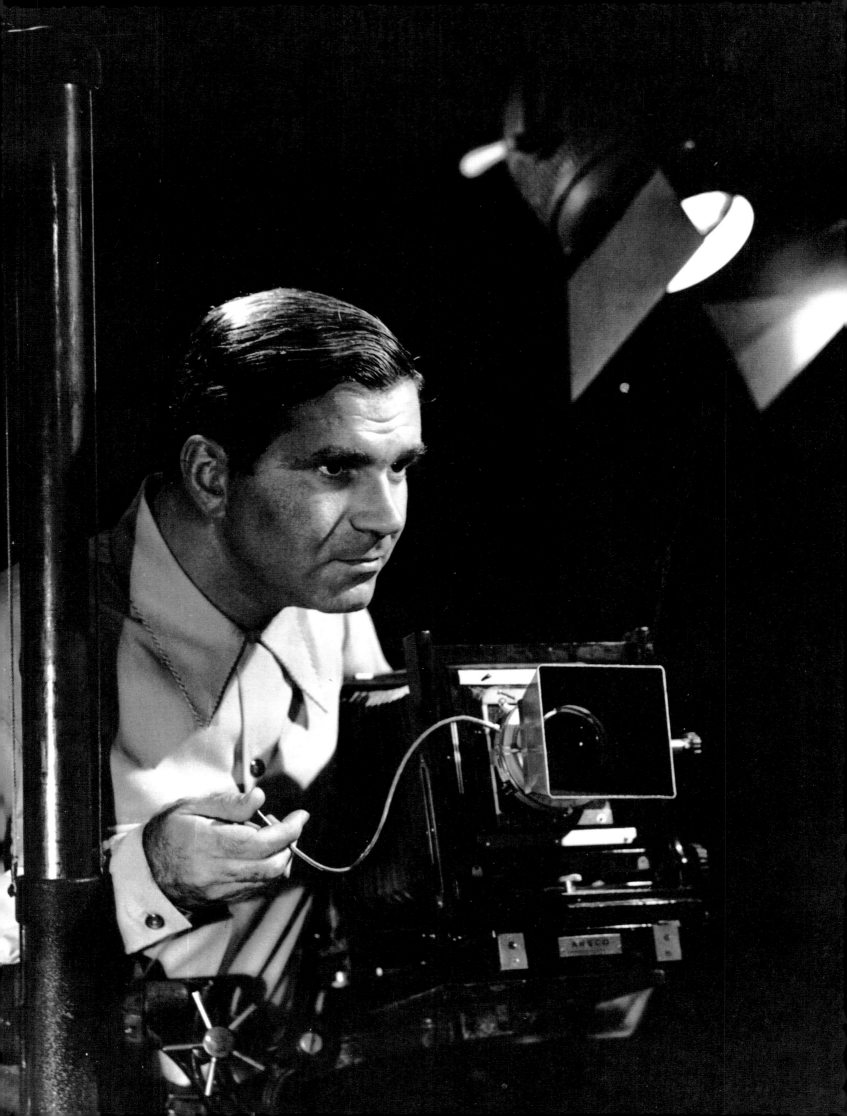

Portrait of My Dad

Dad has been called "the Rembrandt of the photographic portrait," "the King of Hollywood glamour," "the Vargas of pinup photography," "the discoverer of Marilyn Monroe," yet no single phrase can sufficiently paint a portrait of the extraordinary life, the diversity and the innovative genius of my internationally renowned dad, one of the most sought-after photographers of Hollywood's illustrious golden era.

He was a survivor to the core. His dreary childhood in the orphanages of Berlin, the tortures of Nazism, and the loss of loved ones drove him with a vengeance in the midst of fear and chaos to obtain a doctorate in criminal psychology, a privilege allowed to one percent of young Jews. As a leader in the underground Jewish Youth Organization, he was on the Gestapo list facing the door of death. On the eve of his heroic escape to Rio de Janeiro, he sat in the Ufa Palace movie house and was moved by the camaraderie between Gable and Tracy in *San Francisco* as they faced earthquake and fire, and consequently changed his ultimate destination to Berkeley, California, where he completed his studies. Ironically, decades later life would imitate art when Maria Shriver interviewed him on the "CBS Morning News" and asked, "What male star's friendship do you treasure most?" Choked with emotion, he boasted, "Gable, my first star and pal." In Hollywood, he would fight against obscurity as a penniless refugee who faced studio and union brush-offs. In his quest for discovery and acceptance, he became a directorial apprentice under Max Reinhardt's Actors Workshop, which would plant the seed and introduce him to the directorial approach to photography that he later combined with his insights and studies of the human mind to come full circle in understanding the inner, as well as outer, makeup of his subjects.

Despite obscurity and lack of funds, he set up his first darkroom in the basement of his Hollywood apartment in 1940. Shortly thereafter, he moved his studio to the famous Sunset Strip. "No one knew the name Bernard, but they all knew Hollywood," and hence was created the optical trademark signature, Bernard of Hollywood, that ensured visually for decades the image of glamour. Each week he featured a different 30-by-40-inch portrait of a star under his neon-lit signature. During the following years he became the only photographer of his era who simultaneously opened studios in the idyllic oasis of Palm Springs, amidst Laguna Beach's affluent community, and in infamous Las Vegas, where he ran the ultimate portrait salon in the glamorous penthouse of the Riviera Hotel.

In 1984, Hollywood applauded Dad for being the first still photographer to be honored by the Academy of Motion Picture Arts and Sciences with a fifty-year retrospective exhibition of more than 120 of his legendary portraits including Marilyn Monroe, Elizabeth Taylor, Gregory Peck, Marlene Dietrich, Clark Gable, Ginger Rogers, Rita Hayworth, John Wayne, Jayne Mansfield, Leonard Bernstein, Tyrone Power, Brigitte Bardot, and Spencer Tracy. In his moving and unabashed words to the Academy, he

Bruno Bernard self-portrait, circa 1946

1

revealed, ". . . I have never retouched any of my photographs. My aim has been to capture the human essence of my sitters and transfer it to the sensitive emulsion of film, and my definition of the ultimate photographic portrait worthy of the name is a photographic biography of the physical and mental makeup of the sitter and, at the same time, an autobiography of the photographer. . . ."

Under this perspective of my dad's words, this fascinating collection of Norma Jean/ Marilyn focuses on and reveals important and crucial periods of their close friendship and his intimate knowledge of the real Marilyn behind the public role. To assemble this book was, therefore, more than merely recalling negatives and prints from four corners of the

to Bruno Bernard in September, 1954

In 1984, the Academy of Motion Pictures Arts and Sciences honored Bruno Bernard. Seen here with his daughter, Susan Bernard, and his grandson, Joshua Miller.

globe over several years, or gathering, digesting, and editing the essence of my dad's published writings, journal notes, articles, letters, and tapes and retracing my memory of conversations remembered and forgotten. It was an arduous and fascinating journey of psychological probing and unraveling of the portrait of an artist, tracing a world viewed through a lens laced with magic, vanity, and self-proclaimed imagery with Dad focusing on the sight of a woman so alive, so immersed and possessed by ambition and perfection that she lingers in our consciousness over a quarter of a century since she left the stage of life.

Of all the accolades bestowed on Dad, the phrase that gave him the most joy was "This is the discoverer of Marilyn Monroe." He took great pride in his ability to uncover the mysterious photogenic qualities in Norma Jean that transformed a nice-looking girl into a larger-than-life illusionary beauty. Glamour photography has been defined as "making a silk purse out of a sow's ear." However, if it had not been for her almost pathological obsession with becoming a star coupled with her uncanny ability to transform herself before the camera, she would not have become Marilyn and stepped onto the illustrious stage of the beloved goddess's pantheon.

Her luminous image is more alive today than during her lifetime.

Marilyn's presence is everywhere. After Dad's passing, I carried on his legacy of the Bernard of Hollywood Studios, which preserves and publishes his legendary photographs. I was surprised to learn that legacy is also Marilyn's, with the bittersweet realization that Marilyn now belongs to everyone. Her unyielding allure brought both new horizons and battles beyond my wildest imagination.

The literal meaning of the word photographer, according to its Greek origin, is "light writer." I hope with camera and pen this pictorial essay emulates the celebration of Marilyn on the stage of life with the light of compassion.

CHAPTER ONE

Norma Jean

1946–1948

Timing is everything. Or was it destiny that brought the unknown Norma Jean to walk aimlessly past my father just as he was leaving his dentist's office? Filled with dreams, she stared up at Dad's inviting Bernard of Hollywood sign above a life-size portrait of Gregory Peck, and moments later asked, "Mr. Bernard, do you really think I can make it as a model?" And his reply was "Yes." The glow in her heart was ignited.

In one's life there are one, maybe two, crucial moments that can change a life forever, when your adrenaline runs so high you want to burst with excitement and anticipation. In 1946, Norma Jean's moment was her moment of innocence, transition, and transformation. She believed all that was once unobtainable could possibly be achieved, and her inner soul was both delighted and trembling to the core. If one is lucky to have shared and recorded such a crucial moment with someone, all the better. For my dad and Norma Jean, this time would remain in their memory as an intangible bond of friendship that would outlast her marriages and various relationships with other men. My father captured on his legendary lens a moment that was to become Hollywood history, a moment that led to the evolution of Norma Jean's permanent place in American culture as the number-one all-time cinema icon—Marilyn.

"One morning, when I was nine years old, I came home and they had my mother in a strait-jacket tied to a stretcher, and she was crying. I really got frightened. Someone told me she had para . . . paranoid schizo . . . schizophrenia. My grandmother died in one of those asylums. It's way out in Norwalk. You ever been to Norwalk, Mr. Bernard?" Marilyn continued without waiting for my answer. "God, you'll never get me in one of those places." Then there was a pause and her expression became soulful. "On the weekends, when they let her out to come visit me and take me away from the orphanage, she seemed really happy. She'd take me to the movies, and once I got to go to Grauman's Chinese and watch a big Hollywood premiere, and I saw my favorite movie star, Jean Harlow, get out of a big limousine in a beautiful white dress. Then my mother had to go back to that place, and I had to go back to the orphanage."

JOURNAL: While nature has been generous to her figure, her face is just like that of any pretty girl her age—very much the girl next door. With the exception of her translucent skin, her waiflike innocence, the helplessness underneath."

"You see, the orphanage is a whole lot better than the seven foster homes where they had me clean toilets and wash dishes to earn some money. They didn't love me. That was okay. What really got me was out of nowhere, I was brought to this orphanage . . . you know, the one on Vine called the Los Angeles Home Society. I could read and there was this big sign over this great big column, and I hollered, 'You're lying, I'm not an orphan, I have a mother!' I kept crying and crying, but they didn't listen to me and said, 'You have to go in.' 'But I have a mother!' I cried, and they dragged me in, they made me go there. I knew someday I'd get out. I mean there were a lot of kids like me. I guess . . . you know, Mr. Bernard, I used to stand out in the middle of the playground and there was this tall water tower and on the top it said RKO and I'd just stare. Everybody would get mad, 'cause they didn't know what I was staring at."

"And your father, Norma Jean?"

"Well, I'm not really sure who he is. I mean I think I know. . . . There's all these pictures with my mother and this man. She once said he's my father, but then she never wanted to talk about him. I guess one day I've just gotta go look him up and call him."

"If it makes you feel more at ease, I was brought up in an orphanage, but I was not an orphan." Our eyes grew moist, and I continued. "My father came home from World War I with a serious case of asthma, which infected his lungs. He never recovered. Nazis threw hot cement from a window and blinded his eye and he lost his job and became fatally ill. I remember when I was eleven, and as we stood around his death bed, he said to me, 'You are now the father in the family.' There were seven of us. I helped my mother with the pushcart. She was ailing and didn't have the strength or the means to provide for us. Without warning, a social worker took my brother, Heinze, and me to an orphanage because of the pitiful way we lived. This is a great shame in a Jewish family."

"At least you had a family, Mr. Bernard," she wistfully sighed.

"I was alone when I came to America and I was penniless when I kissed the ground on Ellis Island. Hitler's gas chambers took the family I loved. We are survivors, you and I, and Norma Jean, you can embrace the American dream."

JOURNAL 1946: From this moment on, I've become her big brother and father confessor. We are on the same spiritual wavelength. She seems not promiscuous, but a child-woman in search of limitless love and protection as a shield for her vulnerability. She has confessed to me that she has been looking for some human being with whom she could discuss her hopes and problems; one who would not take advantage of her.

"Would you please climb up on the front girder, so that I can get a better angle on your legs?"

"Oh, you want to make a Vargas Girl out of me—all legs and a shrunken head. I know what you're up to, Mr. Bernard."

"What's wrong with the Vargas Girls?"

"Not a thing. I wish I could look like his Ziegfeld beauties in *Esquire*. They're divine. But no real girl could look like those drawings, could she?"

"Not quite. But a photographer can create a similar illusion by elongating the legs from a low perspective . . . but not so low as to distort the proportion of the head too much."

JOURNAL: Up until this morning, I have never seen a model, beginner or pro, who is so at ease before the camera. Norma Jean seems to have a sixth sense between the optical interplay of subject and camera. Concentration, projection and synchronization are second nature to her. The session today was more like a fast game of Ping-Pong than work. I noticed how she contorted her body, urging me to press the shutter before she would lose a

strenuous pose. Her enthusiasm and tenacity are infectious. After hours of continuous shooting, she was still fresh.

JOURNAL: Norma Jean needs a female role model. The loss of her mother has burdened her with the task of mimicking. Therefore, she is a self-taught expert mimic, which all the other photographers I've referred her to can attest to. With childlike gusto she can slip into other people's getups and characteristics and caricature her glamorous role models a bit, either intentionally or unintentionally. If she were to become an actress, this could cause problems.

"I want to become a movie star!" she declared, swirling her hips. "It's been my dream since I was a kid. You've got to help me, Bernie," and she quickly took out my publicity brochure and repeated every word. " 'Professional photography has as its prime purpose selling an actor or a professional performer to producers, directors and, of course, the public.' You've got to take a few more sexy photos of me," she insisted, making boring obscene gestures. "That will be my 'open sesame' to the studios."

"Norma, darling, whatever you do, never put hot on hot—that looks vulgar and would turn a real man off. Let your curves tell it all, and counteract the body language with a complete look of innocence. Your eyes should be asking, 'Why do men look at me?' Blend waif with Venus and you'll create combustion in photos."

Bernard
Hollywood

PORTRAITS · PUBLICITY
9055 SUNSET BLVD.
HOLLYWOOD 46, CALIF.
PHONE: CR. 1·0505

365 S. COAST BLVD.
LAGUNA BEACH, CALIF.
PHONE: 4343

106 PLAZA
PALM SPRINGS, CALIF.
PHONE: 7151

Release: 7/24/46

I hereby permit Bernard of Hollywood to use the pictures he has taken of me for exhibition and commercial use.

Signature:

Norma Jeane Dougherty

JOURNAL: 1946. Gone was the "Jeannie with the light brown hair" and childlike innocence. The new Norma Jean had lightened her hair at the advice of her modeling agency. I couldn't help smiling to myself. I'm so used to hair color as a season affair with my models. Her phony voice reeked of elocution lessons, and threatened to throw an element of strangeness into our hitherto perfect, personal relationship. She even mimicked the headlines in my advertising brochure. Her idea of Miss Glamourpuss: parted lips, her tongue teasing her teeth lasciviously, half-closed eyes reinforcing the irresistible come-hither look. The man in me was not turned on by the performance—the frustrated director in me cautioned her, demanding she change her act. My directions sank in, at least for this sitting, and she changed the French baby-whore look into a variety of child-woman expressions. I've seen the proofs and I'm certain that they will drive the casting directors and producers wild.

"I'm grateful things are really jumping for me as a model, Bernie," Norma declared. "I can't believe you've put me on the cover of all these romance and men's magazines. But, to tell the truth, it gets sort of boring just posing after a while. Even if it does pay the rent."

With co-star Adele Jergens in *Ladies of the Chorus*

Betty Grable

JOURNAL: My friend at 20th Century–Fox, Ben, was so impressed with the color photos I sent him that he met with her today and wants to give her a screen test option. He was struck by her beauty and childlike quality, her inexpensive cotton-print dress encasing her "astonishing figure." Ben and I discussed our mutual concern for her high-pitched voice, and it was decided she should make a silent screen test. I, then, suggested how important it was, if possible, to shoot the test in color, since Zanuck had okayed it based on my color photographs. She needed as much going for her visually as possible, since we were both afraid of the fact that she didn't have any acting training—not even in high school.

JOURNAL: *Prosit!* What timing! *The L.A. Times* today published a photo showing the RKO motion picture magnate, Howard Hughes, in an iron lung clutching the just-released *Laff* magazine color pinup cover I shot on Norma. In an accompanying story the notorious gossip columnist Hedda Hopper wrote, "Howard Hughes must be on the road to recovery, he turned over in his iron lung and wants to know more about the lovely cover girl, Norma Jean." I SOS'ed Darryl Zanuck, "I suggest you sign up the beautiful child-woman, Norma Jean Baker, before Howard Hughes."

JOURNAL: "What a gorgeous girl!" Zanuck declared. "Bernard, we're signing her to a studio stock contract."

"Ben mentioned they're going to have to do something about my name." Then, suddenly, her composure cracked and tears rolled down her freshly made-up face and she began to weep compulsively, shaking her head in disbelief at the good news. "I still can't believe it. I'm so grateful to you, Bernie," and, she continued, "what about my grandmother's name, Monroe?"

"Such as in President James Monroe, the father of the Monroe Doctrine?"

"Oh, Bernie, you're so intelligent."

"Miss Monroe, may you remember the wise writer, André Maurois, who said, 'Si vous atteignez au succes, gardez la qualité qui vous a apportée le succes.' 'If you attain success, retain the qualities that brought you success.'"

"You discovered me, you believed in me; I'll always remember everything started with you."

JOURNAL: Marilyn bit her lip, silently pledging to me, Oh, Bernie, every day on the lot I pass Betty Grable's swell dressing room and get this pain in my heart, and I promise myself that one day, I'll get a dressing room like hers and the GI's are gonna send me oodles of letters.

JOURNAL: Marilyn is diligently attending her elocution, pantomime exercises in the drama barracks on the Fox lot. However, I'm concerned that she's spending more time than she should in their photo studios and mine, preoccupied with shooting thousands of photos, the so-called cheesecake and leg-art that the studio sends out to whet the public's appetite, using the more attractive than talented stock contract bit players whose movie parts eventually land on the cutting room floor. In my studio today, she continues to mimic all the poses of Grable and increases their range and impact with her youthful sex appeal, inventiveness, and instinctive know-how of provocative poses.

JOURNAL: I picked her up at the studio, since her car, an old secondhand Ford, is usually at the repair shop. Marilyn confessed her fears and anxieties concerning her movie contract; she's aware of the fragility of the situation. And, she has a premonition of being fired because of her lack of acting ability.

JOURNAL: Marilyn has not been returning my phone calls. "Mr. Bernard, she just stays in her room, lays down on her bed and cries, she hasn't been hardly eating or talking to anyone. She won't even comb her hair. She just keeps crying as if to drown Marilyn," one of the girls at the Hollywood Studio Club related. She was dropped by Fox. The dream world Marilyn had erected with such inventiveness and persistence had suddenly collapsed her basic insecurities through this initial shock. As I feared, Marilyn was also neither professionally nor personally prepared for the big studio "buildup."

"Who's going to give me another chance after Fox dropped me like a hotcake?"

I replied, "I came to Hollywood and I knew no one and I couldn't even get into the unions. So, I became an apprentice to the great director Professor Max Reinhardt, and it was only then that I started to absorb the art of directing. I'm going to introduce you to Natasha Lytess. We met during my Reinhardt days. Fortunately for you she is now the head drama coach at Columbia Studios. She could be your Reinhardt."

Ciro's on Sunset

JOURNAL: There was another factor contributing to Marilyn's dismissal. It's Marilyn's bad luck that Zanuck is more receptive to exotic beauties than to blondes, which is my observation of his personal tastes. This weakness was confirmed to me only today by my dear friend, Aquanetta, the illustrator Harry Clive's wife, also a great exotic beauty, who told me, "Ben said Zanuck wanted to see me in his office. He waved me impetuously to a low chair in front of his throne. Before I could say 'Jack Robinson,' he had opened his zipper and cracked his big prick down on the desk, 'Gimme a good blow-job, you black witch, and you won't have to worry about good parts. I'm going to make a star of you.' I ran out of his office as if stung by a wasp. It was the end of my motion picture career."

"Bernie, you must show me your proofsheets of Lili St. Cyr," Marilyn announced with great gusto as she ran into the studio. "You told me she's the most glamorous strip-tease artist of all time. Can you take me along with you to her opening at Ciro's tonight?" Marilyn pleaded. "I must study her every move. I've got an audition at Columbia for a role in *Ladies of the Chorus*. I would play the daughter of a former burlesque star, who becomes a burlesque queen. Sounds like something I could do, huh?"

JOURNAL: We sat ringside in the plush club along with Eleanor Roosevelt and Humphrey Bogart, while the police stood guard contemplating a raid. Religiously, Marilyn watched every movement on the stage as the soft light glowed down on Lili's statuesque, exquisite body as she lowered herself into the $18,000 bathtub. Norma Jean was mesmerized by Lili's beauty and considered her performance a truly great work of art.

Lili St.Cyr on stage

JOURNAL: Marilyn's mimicry of Lili combined with her ingenious vulnerability paid off. She's landed the role in *Ladies of the Chorus*, her first part of any length, and a stock contract at Columbia to boot. Natasha, as I predicted, was taken by Marilyn's candor and self-deprecation. Within a short period of time, she became the staunchest believer in Marilyn's potential as an actress. Marilyn realizes that Natasha's opinions are backed up by years of experience in the theater. She has moved in with Natasha and spends her evenings in Natasha's home with members of the European theatrical community, former members of the Reinhardt repertory company. Natasha has taken a genuine interest in Marilyn's private life and become her shield against the outside world, a surrogate mother. Natasha understands and sympathizes with her deep-seated inferiority complex and gives her the training and support she desperately needs.

The Birth of Marilyn

1949–1950

Marilyn confessed to Dad that she had second thoughts over the nude calendar assignment she'd shot for Tom Kelly. During this period, Columbia's star buildup came to a halt. She was again feeling hopeless, and just happened to drop into Dad's studio, looking for another modeling assignment. Her arrival came in a timely fashion. He had been commissioned to do a cover layout story on his favorite stomping grounds in the Springs.

The Palm Springs Racquet Club was a divine and cherished private hideaway of the Hollywood colony, offering a Shangri-la close enough, and yet far enough, from the stress and strain of the studios. Ralph Bellamy and Charles Farrell, its founders, impregnated it with a carefree, short-sleeved atmosphere. The exclusive playground forbid cameras, and only Dad was given photographic privileges since he was on a first-name basis with the stars. It was in Palm Springs one auspicious morning that the then unknown Marilyn was unloaded along with the camera equipment from my father's station-wagon. The photo safari would change the course of her life forever.

JOURNAL: The tennis courts were swept clean when the voluptuous Marilyn posed in her body-hugging swimsuit and four-inch cork heels on the diving board. After a few shots I heard behind me, "Hello, Bernie. Leave it to you to unearth new talent each week. This time you've surpassed yourself. Who's this gorgeous dame . . . your girlfriend?" I knew at that instant this could only have been Johnny Hyde, a vice president at William Morris, a shrimp in stature, but long in connections. I felt annoyed at what he was implying. He asked if I would mind his taking a few snapshots for private use. Of course, he didn't wait for an answer and made a quick dash to his bungalow and stormed out with a Leica and several telephoto lenses, to the amusement of our pals, who know he's a former circus acrobat turned agent. He crouched on his belly and clicked away from his frog perspective, as if Eastman Kodak was going out of business. After I revealed who this "jerk of a guy" was, I might as well have packed up my camera gear. It was Johnny's show. On one level I was happy for Marilyn that he was interested in her, and, on the other hand, he had rudely interrupted my assignment. Over lunch, Johnny had a "great" idea. "Do you mind, Bernie, old boy, if I take Marilyn to Papa [Joseph] Schenck's tonight?" Of course, Marilyn in her pleasant shrewdness left the decision up to me in spite of our prior invitation to join Sy Bartlett and Elizabeth Taylor for dinner at the Racquet Club, where I had made special

Palm Springs Racquet Club

With Johnny Hyde at the Racquet Club

reservations. I encouraged Marilyn to go to Schenck's house with Johnny. I know she will meet some producers and directors who could end her present state of unemployment.

JOURNAL: On Monday, Johnny was on the phone convincing John Huston to test Marilyn for *The Asphalt Jungle*. So ambitious is Marilyn she's been studying her lines with Natasha in seclusion, line by line, word by word. Natasha promised her she'd quit her job at Columbia to coach her on the set if she got the part. I did a little investigation and casually dropped in next door on my old pal Paul Kohner, Huston's agent. "On the first take," Paul laughed, "the girl had the part. Falsies or no falsies."

"Johnny says I could become the representative of my time like Clara Bow or Jean Harlow."

JOURNAL: Johnny would not permit me to take any more pictures of Marilyn in a two-piece bathing suit, which, ironically, had endeared her to him only a few months before. "Bernie, I know you can understand. I want to make a serious actress out of her and pinups would be counterproductive to my buildup," he lectured. "However, just out of friendship, I'm going to let her pose for only you in a one-piece." On the other hand, he is giving no false notion about her potential. He didn't compare her to Garbo or Duse. He speaks of hard work and apprenticeship rather than of genius. He has made her realize that the right director and cameraman are more important than all her co-stars combined.

JOURNAL: Now, with Johnny solidly backing her up in every way, she's suddenly maturing and incapable of panic or hysteria. There are glimmers of an elusive spirit inhabiting Marilyn. She's under the pretense that the past defeats and frustrations have lost their sting. After she had lunch at Romanoff's with Johnny, she drove up in her shiny new red convertible sports car wearing one of the new outfits from the many boxes stacked up in the backseat. A cosmetic surgeon in the Springs had restyled her nose and straightened the facial tissues under her skin. Under his tutelage, the changeover from the natural nice girl next door to the siren, Marilyn, was complete.

JOURNAL: The indefatigable Johnny obtained a copy of a very rough uncut version of Marilyn's scenes in *Asphalt Jungle* and projected the film for his pal Joe Schenck in his private penthouse. Schenck gave it to Joe Mankiewicz, the director, who hired Marilyn to play Miss Caswell in *All About Eve*. Even though the lines are few and her exposure would be limited to two or three scenes, Johnny and Natasha assured her that it would be better to play a minor role than wait for a more important one in a film directed by a less talented and respected director.

With Bette Davis and George Sanders in
All About Eve

"When I was in my dressing room reading the book of sonnets by Rainer Maria Rilke you gave me, Mr. Mankiewicz interrupted and was very patronizing. He asked me, 'How come you're reading Rilke of all people. . . . Do you know who he is?'"

"How did you respond?"

"I told him, 'He's a German poet, of course.' And then he persisted and asked, 'What makes you select such an esoteric writer?' I couldn't answer, I felt so bad. I just pulled out all your favorite books with English translations, C. F. MacIntyre on Goethe and Rilke and Emma Lazarus on Heine, and looked him straight in the eyes," she painfully giggled, "and asked, 'Is something wrong, Mr. Mankiewicz?'"

Understanding her inferiority complex regarding the gap in her education, I recited a poem:

> *Seldom have you understood me*
> *Seldom have I read your mind*
> *Yet when in the shit we found us*
> *We were of a kindred kind.*

Marilyn laughed out loud, but suddenly tears ran down her cheeks as she spontaneously embraced me.

———————

JOURNAL: Johnny is pressing Marilyn to marry him. Johnny senses Marilyn's absolute dependence on the security he has given her. He senses she'd be fatally wounded if success didn't come to her. What he doesn't know is the creature he is creating and whose recognition he is attempting to ensure could come apart if she realizes that success is simply not enough. He asked me to intercede, thinking my paternal attitude with Marilyn might be a decisive factor in changing her mind about marriage. Marilyn has refused, knowing of his heart condition. Many starlets in town are gold diggers and would have jumped at the opportunity. She is a decent human being.

"I love Johnny, but I'm not in love with him. . . . What does it all add up to if you don't have respect for yourself? If there's one thing in my life, Bernie, I want to be said of me, it's that I never was a kept woman."

———————

JOURNAL: December 1950. In the same week that Johnny's heart surgeon warned him to slow down, he accelerated his pace and convinced 20th Century–Fox that Marilyn has become "a fine dramatic actress, too," and today secured her a seven-year contract with Fox. She will star in *As Young As You Feel. All About Eve* won four Academy Awards, including Best Picture. The public is taking notice of Marilyn. A world premiere is being planned for *Asphalt* in June.

———————

"He's got all these tubes running through him, and they've got him under a big oxygen tent," she blurted out.

"Who, Marilyn, who?"

"Johnny. He had a heart attack at the Racquet Club. I'm calling from Palm Springs."

"Did you call his doctor in L.A.?"

"Yes, uh . . . uh . . . I'm going to follow the ambulance back to Cedars."

"Marilyn, listen to me carefully," I said slowly. "You are not in a state to drive. Tell the attendant that you insist you must come back in the ambulance with him."

"If anything happens to Johnny," Marilyn whispered, her voice beginning to crack, "I can't go on without him."

CHAPTER THREE

The Goddess

1951–1953

In the early fifties, light years before the so-called sexual revolution, when artistic freedom was stifled and powerful censorship bureaus and courts ruled, Marilyn emerged on the platform of sexuality. Liberated before her time, she and my father joined forces and won battles for freedom of expression: Dad defending and winning cases in the puritanical courts of Boston and pioneering the novel approach to the art of pinup photography along with Vargas and others, daring to prove "a nude need not be perceived as a vulgar display of the feminine body, but rather as a legitimate work of art transmitting aesthetic values," as, to artistic acclaim, Hearst distributed the pre-*Playboy Pinups . . . A Step Beyond*, while Marilyn raced from one film to another and became the number one Dreamgirl of the American male, the sort of sex symbol who made the lonely GI Joes swoon, giving them something very concrete worth fighting for. Marilyn gave the Fox studio an obstacle course of how to transmit the sexuality of her infamous nude calendar into a flesh and blood person on the screen, in contrast to her counterpart in Europe, Brigitte Bardot, whose love goddess myth was permitted to emerge on screen without censorship. The conflict of the fabricated myth left Marilyn in a constant state of anxiety and confusion over her identity. And all this time women watched the hip-swinging child-woman in all her vulnerability preach Parker's "Men never make passes at women who wear glasses" and wondered how could someone so sexy and powerful be as vulnerable and unconfident as they were.

Brigitte Bardot

MM

JOURNAL: Marilyn was in seventh heaven again—seeing her name up in lights on a motion picture marquee was the best medicine for her after the long months mourning Johnny. Through her photographs she was becoming the best-known unknown player long before becoming a star. She is in such high spirits that she climbed high on the top of a ladder and pointed proudly to her name on the marquee advertising *As Young As You Feel*.

"Look at Marilyn up there," she mused, referring to her motion picture character in the third person. "She's bigger than me. I wish it said Norma Jean, then everybody at the orphanage would know it's me. Soon people will turn their heads when I walk down Hollywood Boulevard and they'll say to each other, 'Yes, that's her, that's Marilyn.'"

JOURNAL: I squeezed her hand and whispered in her ear, "Be Norma Jean," as she plowed her way through the hoards of anxious press. The confession that an eagerly listening nation got from Marilyn's own pouting lips was a tearjerker to the core, from being born out of wedlock and tossed from one loveless foster home to another to taking

As Young As You Feel billboard

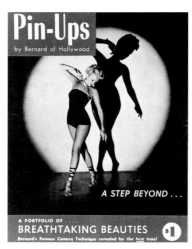

Bruno Bernard publication, 1950

refuge in big Hollywood, unable to pay the rent, to say nothing of the grocery bills, when she allowed Mr. Kelly to talk her into taking the nude calendar assignment. . . . The men and women from the press corps got writer's cramp, their hands racing over their notebooks. The cameramen popped their flashguns in frantic attempts to record every expression of Marilyn's frightened face. Overnight, in the morning papers, Marilyn had become everyone's little sis. The protective instinct in millions of big brothers had been aroused. The good old USA had taken her to their hearts. Thereby turning, as I had suggested, a potential disaster to box office. In my heart I wished she would have dared to take the bull by its horns and tried to combat singlehandedly an inveterate prejudice in people's minds, but she couldn't tell the naked truth.

JOURNAL: *Prosit!* My book *Pinups—A Step Beyond* was published today. My good pal, Vargas, wrote a beautiful commentary and Roy Croft, who's exclusively handling Marilyn's publicity, wrote its introduction. Last week he told me handling Marilyn's publicity is about as easy as guarding a bag of fleas. "In photo sessions, I can never let her out of my sight for fear of her strip-tease inclinations. The moment she spies a press photographer on the lot, she immediately lifts her skirt and falls into a 'cheesecake' pose." I featured Marilyn looking like Norma Jean in *Pinups*. . . . I called it, "Making the Grade." We celebrated the publication over lunch at the Villa Nova and I presented her with one of the first copies off the press. She pensively studied the once unfinished teenager, Norma Jean, as if she were a stranger.

JOURNAL: There is no question that during this period Marilyn did as much, if not more, than her publicity men to build up the sex image. After all, in the meantime, she had inherited Betty Grable's private dressing room on the lot, a dream she had coveted since her days as an unknown. Now she, obviously, enjoyed playing film star Marilyn to the hilt. Unfortunately, she didn't inherit Betty's equanimity begotten by the creative satisfaction of her film work and happy family life.

JOURNAL: For our sitting, she brought a pocket edition of Rilke's *Selected Poems* in MacIntyre's superb translation, which I had given her last year. I was amazed how she started to read in German—in her *Gentlemen Prefer Blondes* Lorelei voice, as she called it—the poem "Madness." The girl in the poem is as mad as Ophelia. Marilyn's selection of this morbid subject seemed strange to me at a time when a bright future seemed to be within her grasp.

"One night I might read my poems to you if you promise not to laugh at me."

"Promise!"

I knew then that Norma Jean was not dead, she was only in hiding under black lace.

JOURNAL: Her next films, *How to Marry a Millionaire* and *Gentlemen Prefer Blondes*, have become box-office hits. The American press agents' brainstorming perfected the first clean sex bomb long before the Pentagon worked on the making of the first "clean" atom bomb. Marilyn seemed to fit into the prefabricated beautiful-but-dumb Hollywood-blonde groove. The exhibitors didn't give a hoot what she played or how, as long as people came to the theaters. No matter how insane the storyline, the legions of fans in the dark of the motion picture houses mentally wrote their own scripts and viewed the stag show of their fantasy overheated by the incendiary bare blonde depicted on their calendars and matchboxes. Her performances were often strip-tease *in perpetuum* with the effects of a delicious aphrodisiac.

Marilyn's star status came with having her hand and footprints cemented on the floor of the picture palace Grauman's Chinese. Her childhood dreams were realized, but what happened to Norma Jean, I questioned. The fierce battle between the two antagonists in her soul were about to unfold.

With Jane Russell at Grauman's Chinese Theater

"This afternoon, I did my first scene with Michael Chekhov from *The Cherry Orchard* in his home," she explained, posing on a stool, cinched in a camisole, the one the public will only get a glimpse of her in when she undresses in *River of No Return*. "You know, Bernie, it was more exciting than to act on any movie set I've ever been on."

"Fantastic! Chekhov is considered one of the greatest acting coaches of our time, part of the Reinhardt ensemble."

"Not so fantastic," she sighed, looking very distraught. "In the middle of our scene, Chekhov suddenly stopped me . . . and looked gently at me. 'May I ask you a question?'" Marilyn mimicked. " 'Anything,' I told him. 'Will you tell me, truthfully, were you thinking of sex while we played the scene?' 'No,' I told him. 'Mr. Chekhov, there is no sex in this scene. I wasn't thinking of it at all.' And then he questioned me real seriously, 'You had no half-thoughts of embraces or kisses on your mind?' I kept repeating, 'No, none.' I insisted I was really concentrating on the scene. And then he started to act very strange and to pace back and forth." Then, Marilyn began mimicking him again. " 'All through the scene I kept receiving sex vibrations from you, as if you were a woman in the grip of passion. Now, I see the difficult problem the studio has. Marilyn, no matter what you are doing or thinking, you give off these vibrations.' Then he was very honest and forthright with me, and said that the studio doesn't care anything about me as an actress, and I'm making a fortune for them by vibrating in front of a camera."

Robert Mitchum promotion for Bernard's *Pinups...A Step Beyond*

JOURNAL: In the photographic and cinematic realm, she had developed a sixth sense for what was photogenic. She treated the camera as if it were her lover to bewitch, bother, and bewilder. She gave herself with total abandon to this lifelong love affair that sometimes was misinterpreted by my colleagues behind the camera as promiscuity, and gave vent to imagined love affairs on a physical plane. As her photographer friend, I always consider myself the stand-in for her emotions and never as the real protagonist of her sexual fantasies.

JOURNAL: Her expressions and moods were as vital as the rush of Niagara. Marilyn was never more vibrant than onstage and backstage at the telethon to raise funds for the Children's Catholic Hospital, a charity close to her heart. Whenever she was near children.

she'd light up and there was an intrinsic emotional response to them. She got deep satisfaction and pleasure helping them and giving them love. When she returned to Hollywood after filming *River of No Return* with Mitchum, she confided to me an episode involving the ten-year-old actor in the cast.

"Tommy would do a scene with me and then he would just run off to his mother without a word. I was real hurt. On the third day, when his mother was not around, I went up to him and said, 'Tommy, could I speak to you for a minute? You've been avoiding me for three days. We've never met before this picture, so I couldn't have done anything to hurt you. What is it?' He just looked at me real frightened and finally said, 'It was my priest, my priest told me that I shouldn't talk to a woman like you when we're not working.' Bernie, I felt like someone had kicked me so hard in the stomach. But then the next week, when Joe came up to see me on the set, Tommy thought he was so great that I must be okay. And you know, Bernie . . . I began to care more for Tommy than any of the co-stars I've ever had."

With Mitchum in *River of No Return*

JOURNAL: Marilyn is now a stricter critic of her performances than most of her critics and fans. Her own misgivings about constantly being referred to as Hollywood's dumb blonde are being reinforced by her baseball-hero boyfriend, Joe DiMaggio. He's unenthusiastic about her public image. This afternoon in the screening room, sitting next to Joe, she became physically ill while viewing her wilderness version of the sexy blonde in *River of No Return* with my old friend, Mitchum. She was so distraught she walked over to Zanuck's office and asked to see him, but was told, "No meeting, just appear on the *There's No Business Like Show Business* set when notified." She and Natasha did secure a meeting with Spyros Skouras, the dollar and cents man at Fox. Her popularity had, after all, grossed the studio over $200 million. She requested from Skouras a complete change of character in dramatic vehicles. "Baby, forget the sentimentalities, you make money only with your tits and ass. . . . Your talent is located above your waist and below your navel." Marilyn was devastated. To her horror, she finally came to the realization that she is a studio commodity. Despite her dedication and tenacity, no one at the studio gave a damn. I suspected all along her rage and frustration was growing. Norma Jean is so unhappy and depressed, I fear for her and suggested she seek professional psychiatric help.

With co-star Richard Widmark on the set of *Don't Bother to Knock*

With her coach, Natasha Lytess

Bernard
of
Hollywood

Persona

1954

W hen *Redbook* urged Dad to accept *The Seven Year Itch* cover-photo story on Marilyn in New York, they were aware of their personal relationship. He was anything but pleased to shoot in what he referred to as the "humid asphalt jungle." Not only did he not desire to leave his Hollywood oasis, he was anticipating with great excitement shooting Marlene Dietrich's opening in Las Vegas, whom he considered Marilyn's predecessor in the realm of having a sixth sense for what was photogenic.

Dear Bernie,

I'm so happy and in love. Joe and I are in Japan on our honeymoon. He's a real good guy and a gentleman, and sometimes a little shy. I've decided for sure that it'll be better if I only make one or two more films after I shoot There's No Business Like Show Business *and then retire to the simple good life of a housewife and, hopefully, mother. Joe wants a big family. He was real surprised when we were met at the airport by such gigantic crowds and press. He said he never saw so much excitement, not even when the Yankees won the World Series.*

The Department of Defense asked me if I would like to go to Korea to entertain the troops. Imagine me before all those kids in uniform fighting to save America. I'm going to give them a show they'll never forget. See you in Hollywood.

Love,
Marilyn

P.S. Can you meet me in Korea?

Just married to Joe DiMaggio

JOURNAL: Korea. The helicopter flew low over the soldiers on the ground. She lay face down on the floor of the copter, lowering her body outside the sliding door, secured only by two soldiers. The sight of Marilyn dangling from the helicopter, waving and blowing kisses, was astounding, if not frightening. Her appearance before the combat-weary troops was electric. It almost caused a riot when she sang "Diamonds Are a Girl's Best Friend." She felt like it was the high point of her life thus far. "Bernie, I never felt like a star before in my heart. It was so wonderful to look down and see a fellow smiling at me."

When we helicoptered back to Japan, Marilyn's temperature had risen to 104

In Korea, 1954

degrees and she was suffering from mild pneumonia. In freezing weather, in a bare-shouldered dress, she had given the fellows her all. She was Marilyn, the worshipped sex goddess, the fabricated identity, the only one she knew, her own creation, which was not the performance of any of her insipid concocted screen characters, but the creation of Marilyn herself.

JOURNAL: New York—9/14/54. Had it not been for my cover story assignment from *Redbook* magazine and Marilyn, ten horses could not have drawn me to *The Seven Year Itch*.

Damn it. I waited three hours in the midst of a yelling, sweating crowd and a bevy of paparazzi, the kind of photographic spectacle I take pride in never being part of. Suddenly, the crowd was yelling in orgiastic proportions. Marilyn, in person, appears. When the director, Billy Wilder, said, "Roll it," Marilyn exits from the theater and goes four steps to the left, stopping directly over the subway grate. At this moment, a subway train is supposedly leaving the station, blowing Marilyn's skirt up high. (For more controllable action the prop men had substituted a wind machine directly under the grate for the train.) In some of the takes, Marilyn's pleated white skirt blew right over her head, to the delight of the howling spectators. According to the script, all Marilyn had to say while enjoying the cool breeze was, "Ah, what a relief. Isn't it delicious!"

The scene was repeated thirty times; Marilyn was fluffing her lines. She wore only slightly transparent white silk panties under the skirt. To the bystanders, it was evident that she was not blonde all over. I refuse to retouch my photos. DiMaggio, standing next to Walter Winchell, was watching the exhibition directly across from me. I could see DiMaggio's embarrassment turning to anger. Quickly, I edged my way across the crowd, hoping to calm him down. Before I reached him, he'd steamed off in a huff. Winchell, whom I owed a lot to for coining me, in his column, "the Rembrandt of photography" while reflecting on my Palm Springs series on Gable, gave me a big hello and said DiMaggio was off to "cool off his Italian macho temper at Toots Shor's." Roy Croft joined us. "We should be glad she's not bottomless. Remember when the gal used to walk around without panties, and Papa Schenck gave her two dozen monogrammed with MM initials?" DiMaggio's absence didn't phase her, and the love goddess continued her endless retakes of the scene, giving her director and her ecstatic public—the average Joe-schmoe, the unemployed loafers, the guys at the bars, the kids on their way to high school—who had gotten up at 6:00 A.M. on a humid day in New York—their money's worth.

When the exasperated Wilder again began explaining the simplicity of the scene, Marilyn discovered me and winked me over, embracing me spontaneously. "Bernie, what are you doing here?" she asked in her famous breathless whisper. And then she added, so the whole crew within earshot could hear, "*Remember, Bernie, you started it all!*"

"Joe seems so lost. He's just so angry with himself, not with me, but with himself and what's happening with us. He thinks he needs to be my chaperone," she rambled on as we went back inside the Trans Lux Theatre, where Alan "Whitey" Snyder was waiting for the touchups. "Milton Greene's going to take care of things. We're going to form Marilyn Monroe Productions. We'll show Twentieth who Marilyn really is. After we finish your portrait for *Redbook*, maybe, Bernie, you can stay on. Milton's coming over; with your legal background maybe you can help me go over the papers he's bringing."

"Marilyn, I don't think you should make any rash decisions and sign anything," I pleaded. "Your marriage is on the line. Remember what I've always told you. Even from afar, my family—Ruth and Susan—are my moral support and Joe is yours."

"I love Joe, Bernie, and I always will. He'll understand. He's the one who's been so embarrassed about all the abuse Twentieth gave me. Big breasts, big ass, big deal. I've had it!"

"You may win your battle with the studio, but you'll lose with Joe."

It was the emotional bond that Marilyn had to her public, the ordinary people, the guys in uniform—the working class, those who struggled through wars and the Depression, whose poverty was no shame—that drove Marilyn. They were her public and, like myself, she would never let them down.

JOURNAL: I really need this portrait sitting of Joe and Marilyn to tie in the cover with my layout. From the hall outside their suite at the St. Regis, I could hear a heated quarrel followed by her hysterical crying. I left, and I never got my sitting. Without a suitable cover photo, my *Redbook* editor would ax the layout. I was downcast and silent. Roy ran into me in the elevator and attempted to console me. "All is not lost, Bernie, old pal, because the outside noise was so loud, Wilder has decided to reshoot the entire scene in Hollywood."

JOURNAL: Back in Hollywood, Marilyn's been heavily sedated. I haven't been able to reach her on the phone, or break through the cordon of her retinue. Days are passing without a response from her. In the meantime, the Trans Lux Theatre and the adjoining Lexington Avenue stores are being rebuilt on the Fox lot. I'm beginning to get concerned, not only about a set appointment for my cover portrait, but about Marilyn's fragile emotional state now being manipulated by self-serving strangers. I'm sending to her home a set of her color Norma Jean first sitting as a memento. I'm writing a message, our familiar Maurois aphorism, "When you attain success, retain the qualities that brought you success."

JOURNAL: "Sorry, Bernard, no dice for a formal portrait," the head of the publicity department, Harry Brand, phoned. "We're lucky if we can finish the picture the day after tomorrow. Billy has ordered a closed set. Out of Marilyn's request and *Redbook*, you will be the only photographer permitted on the set tomorrow." Disheartened and encouraged, I

Bernard's wife, Ruth Brande Bernard

raced to Fox this morning, only for the guard at the gate to tell me they'd axed that day's shooting. I phoned Marilyn's house and the publicity department. No one answered. Feeling completely dejected, I drove home, unconsciously taking the route via Palm Drive, and saw the biggest assembly of Hollywood press I had ever seen in my Hollywood career. I quickly parked my car and raced with my camera to find the sad news that Marilyn would be coming out of her home any minute to announce her separation or divorce from Joe. Marilyn emerged pale as the driven snow, hugging the arm of attorney Jerry Giesler. Since I had come too late to secure a good position, news reporters and photographers were in front of me. I held my Rollei over my head to sadly record Marilyn's goldfish bowl existence. I quickly jumped into the little space left by the black Cadillac parked at the curb to take my "definitive" picture of Norma Jean/Marilyn. Before the car started, I reached through the window and pressed her hand firmly without uttering a word.

We understood each other momentarily as we had so often in the past. As Marilyn listlessly withdrew her hand to dry her tears—real ones, not glycerine—I shot the naked human creature behind the goddess. The fragile doll of Offenbach's *Tales of Hoffmann*. It was the beginning of the end.

JOURNAL: When the green light blinked at the iron door of the huge Stage 3 on the Fox lot and I could enter the set, I saw an exact replica of the Trans Lux Theatre and the adjoining storefronts. Billy Wilder, this time without his Tyrolean hat but with the inevitable riding crop in hand, was giving Marilyn some specific suggestions for the thirty-fifth retake of the skirt-blowing scene. The personified love object was supposed to purr her words contentedly, expressing with each syllable the relief felt from the wind coming through the grate. While her stand-in was wearing long black toreador pants to prevent her from getting a cold, poor Marilyn had nothing on but thin silk panties. Now, she was purring for the thirty-sixth time, "Isn't it delicious. What a relief!"

"Cut. Let's print this one, but one more for perfection," commanded Billy Wilder.

While Marilyn's hairdresser combed her hair, this strange entr'acte of an odd couple, with Natasha prompting Marilyn, resembled more the rehearsal for a marionette show than the shooting of a film scene. In the final analysis it was "absurd theatre" within the make-believe world of movieland and was infinitely more interesting to watch than the edited film on screen.

After the thirty-ninth take of the skirt-blowing scene was in the can, the exhausted Billy Wilder commended Marilyn highly for her staying power. "Great, Marilyn, don't worry one bit. We've printed it, just one more to make it perfect!" Like in a burlesque sketch, everything was repeated from A to Z, the only difference being that the second banana didn't get the meringue pie in his face when the director yelled "Action." At the fortieth take, the director shouted enthusiastically: "Cut! Print it! This is it!"

A nod by Wilder to his assistant brought the megaphone guy into action. "Let's all wrap it up, boys!" From behind the camera Natasha came running towards Marilyn, embracing her jubilantly, while the star, looking lost like a helpless child, asked her, "Do you really think I got it the last time? . . . letter perfect, I mean? or . . ."

"No question in my mind, darling," assured Natasha, "this was it!" Only then did Marilyn seem to awake from her trance and become the bubbling, carefree Norma Jean of olden days.

In her large dressing room a small victory celebration started. Roy Croft uncorked a bottle of Dom Perignon, Marilyn's favorite champagne, and all the members of her permanent staff, her makeup man "Whitey" Snyder, her hairstylist, and her seamstress toasted first their superstar boss and then each other. The prop men and the electrician stormed into the dressing room with fan photos of their number-one star in hand, clamoring for autographs to have a tangible souvenir in remembrance of their Love Goddess.

I used this *lucidum intervallum*—the lucid moment in between her depressive moods—to quickly get an unusual photograph of Marilyn showing her sense of humor. When Sid Skolsky barged into the dressing room gushing with compliments about her performance, I asked Marilyn to pose for me as diminutive Boswell à la Monroe, the moniker Sid had coined for his column. Marilyn instantaneously threw herself on the couch, caricaturing "a motion picture star on Sunday." Any viewer of this photo and the one on the set with Natasha can see clearly how close behind the Marilyn facade was hidden the insecure, unwanted Norma Jean, whose aggressive behavior was surfacing and causing havoc. Fortunately, I was able to capture this merry scene, which showed the smiling, vibrant Marilyn celebrating. Deep down she was in pain. A brief remission, disguising it using the best medicine, humor. That can best be described when we all later descended to the projection room.

Marilyn sat between Sid Skolsky and me, two rows in front of Wilder and his collaborator, I. A. L. Diamond. On the screen rolls the rather (for that period) daring bath scene from *The Seven Year Itch*. While luxuriating in the foam bath, Marilyn's toe gets caught in the faucet. The plumber, played by the fine character actor Victor Moore, is so bewitched by Marilyn's luminous beauty that he drops his wrench in the bathtub. In total embarrassment he tries to retrieve the tool, his hands fumbling a long time under the foam. At this moment Wilder whispers to Diamond, "Too bad we'll have to cut this scene out because of the damn Hays office." Whereupon Marilyn turns around and whispers, "You've got to leave the scene in, Billy, it's the cleanest one in the whole picture."

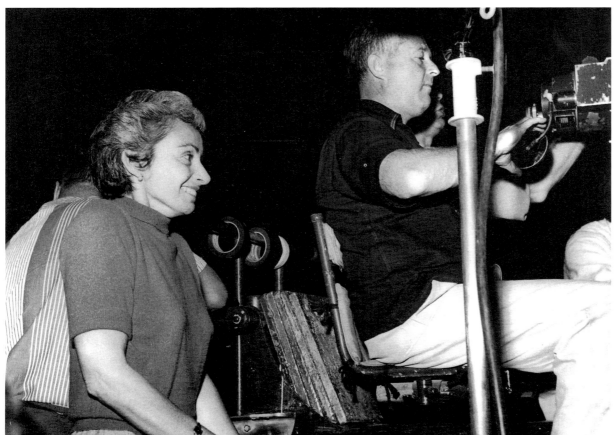

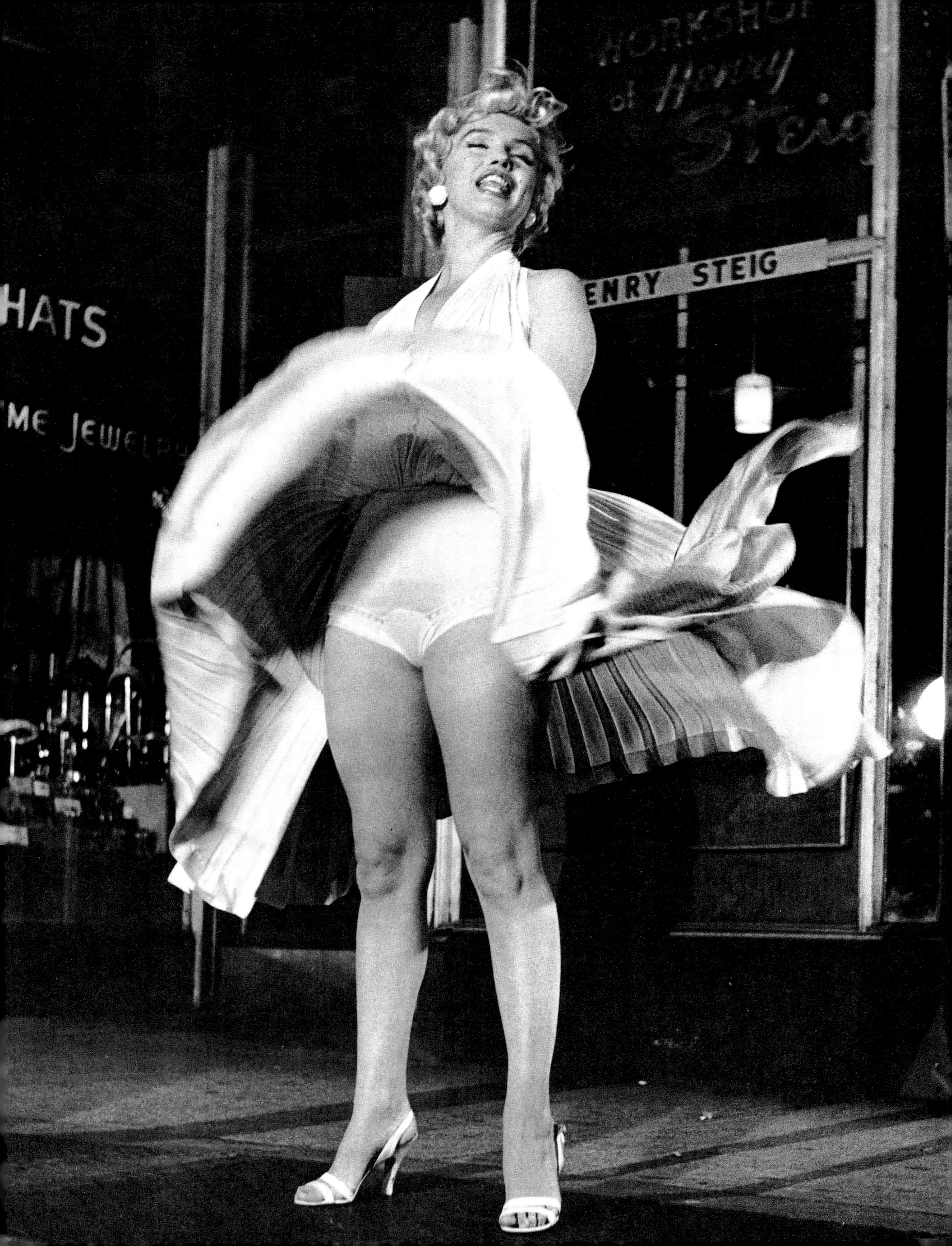
HATS
ENRY STEIG

Renaissance

1955–1962

Where is Marilyn?

Without leaving a forwarding address with Dad, she flew to New York under the name Zelda Zonk, moving her dreams and ambitions with her. In many ways it was the most intelligent and courageous thing she ever did. And she fell madly in love with a part of herself that had never been developed. With sheer guts she embraced the Strasberg's Actors Studio, where the ambiance was hard core—get down to work and plunge into the darkness of your inner self. The artist and the woman, Marilyn, was emerging. On the steps of Washington, she would stand and fight for her belief in the Bill of Rights and her new husband's honor to survive the dreaded McCarthy hearings. She had taken a big risk and turned her back on Fox in a series of legal battles to demand more money, approval of directors, better scripts and, more importantly, respect. After winning the war with Hollywood, she would battle her own terrifying disintegration process.

"Strasberg insists that I enter professional psychiatric treatment, so that I can better discover my inner self. He stresses the 'Method.' I must as an actress find my inner identification with the character, draw from my personal memories and experiences."

"I admire your dedication for self-improvement," I commended. I have observed many of my clients who were under the Strasberg spell arrive in Hollywood, and, without his direction, as independent agents they were unable to do a movie scene until they grasped the 'inner key.'"

"Lee and Paula make me feel I'm part of the family."

"There's a difference between friendship and the attitude of the Strasbergs, who make you believe you belong to them."

JOURNAL: 1956. I envision her walking the streets of New York under dark glasses in disguise, analyzing and analyzing what she believes will "free her" in such a way that her new acting classes are now taking on an almost hypnotic dimension.

JOURNAL: New York. Two hundred reporters and photographers showed up at the Waldorf-Astoria today for the announcement of the historic teaming of Marilyn and Sir Laurence Olivier in *The Prince and the Showgirl*, he representing high art and she photogenia from the rear. She purred to Olivier that he was her favorite actor and hero, and Olivier in a cavalier fashion called Marilyn a brilliant comedienne. Suddenly her gown

With Laurence Olivier at New York press
conference for *The Prince and the Showgirl*

shoulder-strap broke, sending gasps at the prospect of an even more exciting revelation. I can't help but wonder if Marilyn had planned it. She coquettishly requested a safety pin. Flashbulbs popped. A reporter from *Time* asked if she wanted to do *The Brothers Karamazov*, and, if so, what part would she want to play. Marilyn replied she wanted to play Grushenka, since she's the only girl. *One* of the supposed geniuses asked if she could spell Karamazov. Her eyes helplessly met mine. There was a titter of laughter. Thus, the great Olivier was introduced to what Marilyn liked to refer to as "the zoo."

"Bernie, if I'm going to marry a Jewish man, I want to become one. I want Arthur's family to think of me as one of the 'mishpooka.'"

"You mean one of the clan, the family," I said during one of our photo sessions.

"Right, not as a 'shiksa.' I wish I could speak all the languages you do, Bernie, but I had such a rotten education. Thank God Arthur is truly intelligent, beyond what I'd hoped for." Her eyes sparkled and she glowed like a young girl discussing a first love. "We spend so much time lying in bed and reading to each other. I trust him completely and he feels sort of obligated to defend me as an artist. He writes. I cook. I hope to have a son, a man just like Arthur."

JOURNAL: February 2, my birthday, Marilyn's return to Hollywood after a year and a half exile. The phenomenal box office success of *The Seven Year Itch* has put her in the driver's seat. As for myself, I was astonished at the unyielding international requests for my photographs of Marilyn's infamous billowing flying skirt, which was slowly becoming the most visual image synonymous with Hollywood. Today in *The L.A. Times*, Joshua Logan, her new director on *Bus Stop*, expressed, "I wasn't really sure about this Marilyn who was funny and did musicals for Fox, until Strasberg assured me she was the greatest artist since Brando." I thought the comment rather self-aggrandizing, since it was Marilyn who had to approve him. In her revised contract with Fox it gives her the right to reject any film that in her opinion is not "first class," and the same applies to directors and cameramen. Her inner battle is in remission. She is guaranteed high-level artistic freedom, the prerequisite for her long-dreamed-of career as a serious actress. If she has developed into the actor I believe she can be, *Bus Stop* is the vehicle that will prove that she is able to transfer her inner turmoil creatively, instead of aggressively.

Dear Bernie,

I'm terrified. We had to secretly escape from the farm.

We may have to postpone our plans until we get through this ugly political sabotage. The House Subcommittee is giving Arthur only ten days to reveal names or face a contempt citation which could go to the Grand Jury. If they find him guilty, they could give him a year in jail. Arthur won't testify and betray his friends. Who do those guys in Washington think they are anyway? Hitler? That witch hunt, that Un-American Activities Subcommittee. Arthur calls them a "subterranean machine destroying the souls and lives of artists." They and the Hays Bureau should be buried alive. Those hypocrites who probably read dirty books and put them under their pillows at night. How brave you are, Bernie, to have survived after everything you love was dehumanized and destroyed under Hitler's persecution. I now understand a little.

"Bernie, sorry to call you so early . . . you've known me longer than anybody in London . . . can you imagine Professor Reinhardt telling any of his actresses, 'Be sexy. . . . That is what this English Sir Olivier just told me, of all people, in front of the entire crew! That's the same as if he would tell the Pope, 'be pious.'"

"But, Marilyn," I tried to get a word in edgewise, "he probably meant . . ."

"What do you mean 'probably meant'?" she shouted almost hysterically into the telephone. "Either you're sexy, or you're not, you can't fake it. It has to be spontaneous and natural or it becomes a caricature. Do you understand me, can you hear me?"

"I can hear you all right," I consoled calmly, realizing her aggressive state of anxiety was out of control. "And I understand you, as far as I can appraise the situation thousands of miles away. Perhaps it's a misunderstanding. He might have just been teasing you, the world's most famous sex symbol, advising you to throw away the lines—like Reinhardt sometimes does—to offset your obvious body language. Remember my directions in our first study sitting: 'Put sweet on hot.' After all, this great director must know what he's doing. Besides, he is a man and can feel and see that you're oozing sex from every pore of your body."

"Oh, you're all alike," she lamented, a bit of hurt innocence in her tone, "you mistake me for the characters I portray on the screen. I feel that this theatrical nobleman is plain arrogant and wanted to ridicule me, so I will eat out of his hand like the English actors who think he's God. . . . Just because you resemble him enough to play his double," she teased, "doesn't mean you have to take his side."

Photo MM sent to Bernard from London press conference

" 'The angel I married has turned into a self-destructive monster,' " she cried hysterically again over the overseas static. "Arthur wrote this in his secret little notebook."

"Marilyn, it could be just one of his notes for his next play," I said, thinking she'd blown the incident out of proportion.

"It's me, he's writing about me. Arthur's turned against me, and I hate Olivier. They accused Strasberg of exploiting me. He and Arthur don't believe in the Method."

JOURNAL: In this morning's mail, I received a photo of Marilyn, Olivier, and Miller sitting at a press conference with a note on the back, "Dear Bernie, Surprised? I'm playing with your double." Also enclosed is a stack of British newspapers that report on the severe problems on the set of *The Prince and the Showgirl*. The Strasbergs have fueled their egos and offset Marilyn's inbred inferiority complex of working opposite the greatest actor in the English language. Her husband's mental shock treatment is only reinforcing Marilyn's aggressiveness as a shield against her deep-seated insecurity in this depressive stage.

"Arthur's 'tired' of being my nursemaid," she giggled. Her words slurred and sounded intoxicated. "I told him he doesn't have to watch me like a hawk. I need to get my sleep, and I need those pills. He keeps ordering room service not to deliver any bottles of Dom Perignon. Can you imagine? Thank God, my therapist, Dr. Kris, flew in to come to my rescue. He's going to help me get through this horrible nightmare I'm in."

Bernard, circa 1955

JOURNAL: Pregnancy had buoyed up her spirits for a while. She was hoping to be able to lavish the kind of love on her offspring that she herself had longed for as a child. The new surgical operation, involving the cutting of the fallopian tube, dashed her hopes once and for all, aggravating her sense of worthlessness as a woman. Now, even more than before, pills and alcohol became her crutches. Her frequent depressive moods spawned capricious and incomprehensible behavior.

JOURNAL: The burden of Arthur's legal bills persuaded her to accept a role in *Some Like It Hot*.

I discussed the filming with Tony Curtis. He was smoldering: "How would you feel if you had to gnaw forty-two chicken bones in a row just because this dizzy dame couldn't deliver a one-liner? And when an exasperated Billy Wilder informs Jack and me the forty-third take will be printed as long as Marilyn looks good, it makes you feel like an overpaid dress extra."

Those in Marilyn's closest environment are interpreting her new behavior as an outgrowth of an obnoxious personality rather than a pathological mentality.

JOURNAL: Las Vegas. My photo agent wants me to shoot a cover story on Marilyn and Clark Gable. Since Gable recently visited my salon and second home in Vegas, I phoned him first. I didn't want to catch Marilyn in the middle of what I understand are out-and-out scenes openly displayed on the set of *The Misfits* revealing her stormy marriage, which is taking on the dimensions of a Strindberg tragedy.

Clark didn't sound encouraging. "Bernie, boy, right now you wouldn't have a Chinaman's chance. We're weeks behind schedule on account of Marilyn's delays and illness. She is really sick. In her state she shouldn't have even started the picture. Right now, she's not even here, she's in a Los Angeles hospital, drying out. We don't know if, or when, we can finish the picture," Gable said. "Besides, this location has been lousy with photographers. Huston has blown his stack. He asked Eli [Wallach] and me to throw our lassos over a few camera bugs instead of the mustangs, so we can go on shooting around Marilyn. Sorry, I can't give you any better news today. Should anything change here, you'll hear from me. . . ."

JOURNAL: When viewing the rough cut in the projection room of *The Misfits*, Marilyn, sitting next to me, appeared distant and pale. On the screen, she never seemed more fragile or beautiful. When the projectionist rolled the scene where Clark asks Marilyn, "What makes you so sad? You're the saddest girl I've ever met. . . ." Marilyn embraced me and broke down hysterically. Almost compulsively. We comforted one another and not a word was uttered. We had just both suffered a great loss with Clark's sudden passing. For me, it meant the profound loss of a friend whom I owed a great deal to and who would remain forever in my mind as the King. Marilyn's tears were not only the mourning of the man she had admired and had considered her idol since childhood, but they were also the horror and guilt that she couldn't control her new depressive moods and aggressive rampages. They had both caused unbearable tension and delays on the set for Clark. Marilyn's incomprehensible behavior and her surfacing mental illness were the final blows that caused her divorce from Arthur. Complete havoc to her psyche resulted: her unfulfilled goals . . . Hollywood's failure to accept her as a serious actress . . . her continuous attempts at suicide . . . her abortions and unbearable miscarriages . . . her growing fear that her grandmother's and mother's schizophrenic tendencies had caught up with her . . . her drug dependency. . . . The latter was nurtured and encouraged, so Hollywood could get their scene in a lucid moment.

The dark ghosts of Norma Jean had surfaced on the set in the wasteland of Nevada.

JOURNAL: More suicide impulses. Alias Faye Miller-Marilyn is clamoring behind barred windows in the Payne Whitney Psychiatric Clinic, New York. Behind a door which can only be opened from the outside.

> *Dear Bernie,*
>   *I'm not insane. If I stay here any longer, locked up with these poor nutty people, I'm sure I will end up crazy. They will listen to you. You have a doctor's degree before your name. Help me. There must be a better hospital for me. Maybe Joe can help.*
>
>   *Marilyn*

Dr. Kris, who had persuaded her to enter the hospital, ignored my interference. The Strasbergs did not respond right away. Marilyn's hysteria had escalated to such a dangerous pitch they permitted only DiMaggio to transfer her to a private room in the Neurological Institute of the Columbia Presbyterian Hospital.

LADIES
WARDROBE

PICTURE F-73

TITLE Let's Make Love

DIRECTOR G. Cukor

ACTRESS M. Monroe

PART OF Amanda Dell

JOURNAL: London. *Fox Fires Love Goddess Marilyn Monroe.* I was stunned reading the *Daily Mirror* headlines. I imagined hundreds of news reporters descending upon her quaint new hacienda on 5 Helen Drive in Brentwood, stepping not on her vulnerability but on her walkway, where the Latin inscription reads: *Iter meum confectum est* (My journey is over).

. . . "Can Twentieth get the million they're suing for?"

"In the forty-two days of shooting, did you only show up for six?" . . . "Is it true you demanded excessive script changes and were late on the set?" . . .

"Marilyn, can you come to my party and sing 'Happy Birthday'?"

JOURNAL: In spite of her three years studying with the Strasbergs, *The Misfits*, on which she had pinned so much hope as her breakthrough as a serious actress, failed at the box office. She was left feeling out on a limb and emotionally drained at the start of *Something's Got to Give.* Marilyn was declared "expendable." She had lost. Even after her last victory with the studio was won.

JOURNAL: Again, she's ignoring my repeated phone messages, although only a week ago she sent a production still of her walking away and looking back over her shoulder, as if saying to me, "Goodbye."

> *"Sex and seriousness could not exist in the same woman, and this American illness was not about to end."*
>
> —ARTHUR MILLER

Announcing her marriage to Arthur Miller

The Legacy

O n August 5, 1962, the news of Marilyn Monroe's death flashed like lightning bolts around the world. Dad heard it over the radio in Berlin, as he was having lunch in the rooftop restaurant of the Funkturm. A lump formed in his throat and he told the waiter to take away his half-eaten meal and bring him a cup of coffee. His mind raced back over space and time to Marilyn's first sitting. Her whispery child-woman voice—"Mr. Bernard, can you take a few sexy pictures of me?"—echoing in his ears. He expressed how he felt a deep sense of shock. He was upset, since he was unable to help her when she needed him most. He grieved over the loss of the child-woman who was little sis. He fantasized how he could have rushed her to the hospital, where her stomach would have been pumped in time, and he would have brought her back to the living. I imagine the news being broadcast continuously over the radio in the restaurant as Dad felt private pain and saw the impact of the tragic news on the saddened faces of the Berliners. To voice his grief, he immediately called his friend, the editor-in-chief of the *Berliner Illustriete Zeitung*, and told him to hold the presses for his eulogy. He did. Half an hour later, in his *pension*, he dictated an article entitled "Goodbye Marilyn."

. . . Norma Jean/Marilyn, on your crypt we shall not jot down your vital statistics, 37-22-35, as you once suggested in one of your self-deprecating Norma Jean moods. Instead, we will mentally engrave the immortal verse of Goethe, a lifelong admirer of feminine beauty, that reads like poetic prophesy:

> *Distance does not make you complex*
> *you come flying out of breath*
> *to the light that in the end*
> *burns you, butterfly, to death.*

And so the conversations would no longer be. The journal would be closed. There was silence. It was the end of her career and her extraordinary life. In a sense it was a new beginning for Dad. Marilyn's death was the pivotal blow in a decision long brewing, to turn his back on Hollywood. He realized that many of his stars, his close friends, were now gone. Mafia threats on his life forced him to close his Las Vegas salon. The conflict to uphold the aesthetic and ethical values of his profession against the sixties' purely

Collage by Bruno Bernard, circa 1986

Casa Bernards, Palma Mallorca, 1960s

exploitive publishing of "gynecological photographers using three poses . . . each more vulgar than the last," cast even darker shadows. My father sold his four landmark studios to return to his homeland, Berlin, and became a foreign correspondent, covering for *Der Spiegel* the Eichmann trial as a photojournalist. He was so moved by the trial that he began compiling a book, the bestseller *Israel*, and then moved his world to the seclusion of a Mediterranean three-story villa on the pristine beaches of Palma Mallorca, Spain, and plunged into his evolution of artistic and intellectual discovery. And, at the entrance to Casa Bernards, before you took the long journey on pebbled steps, he paid homage to Marilyn and built an enchanted fountain—christening it Norma Jean.

Over the next decades, Dad's social and professional engagements would be ignited by an alternative motive to dispel the rumors and lies over Marilyn's untimely passing. In particular, Dad was certain that "Marilyn was doomed long before she ever met the Kennedys due to her complete detachment from reality."

Robert Kennedy in Rio

JOURNAL: Rio de Janeiro. The occasion is the unveiling of a bust of the late President, John Fitzgerald Kennedy, at the Catholic University in Rio de Janeiro. My reportorial instincts spurred me on to get some reaction to the welter of rumors mushrooming in Hollywood concerning Marilyn's death. At the conclusion of the official unveiling ceremony, highlighted by Senator Kennedy's moving tribute to his assassinated brother, the more carefree atmosphere of the senator's meeting with members of the American Peace Corps in Brazil seemed to offer me such an opportunity.

I approached our celebrated host. "Senator, I believe I am the only Press Corps member present who had the privilege of photographing the late President when he delivered his historic speech, 'Ich bin ein Berliner,' in front of the Schoeneberg City Hall in Berlin."

I could hardly finish my sentence, because I was so emotionally charged. And Robert Kennedy, the man with the reputation of a tough, Irish street fighter, had moist eyes and pressed my hand warmly.

Commenting in a low voice, he said, "I'll never forget that scene as long as I live. The torchlight parade of the Berlin students was, for all of us, the most touching tribute for the late President. I am happy that you managed to be present at that lasting memorial for him and what he stood for."

This totally unexpected human rapport made me tongue-tied. I felt in the grip of a rendezvous with destiny that drowned out all questions of a personal nature about Marilyn at such an historic moment. Instead, without uttering a word, I simply presented him with my favorite portrait of her.

Through Dad's three cancer operations, we spent hours, days, and months unraveling private police files and testimonies and had conversations with dozens who had spent time with her during her last frantic weeks on earth. All the evidence points to the fact that Marilyn did not want to commit suicide. Marilyn died during the night between the fourth and the fifth of August, 1962. Her death was an accident due to a lethal blend of an overdose of Nembutal sleeping pills and alcohol.

In August of 1982, Dad took his eight-year-old grandson, Joshua, to Marilyn's last resting place and laid a bouquet of red roses next to Joe DiMaggio's yellow ones on the twentieth anniversary of her death. It was again through his lens that he best communicated. He placed his camera in Joshua's hands, and directly spoke with Marilyn one last time.

On March 10, 1987, I was astonished to learn how strong Marilyn and my dad's destinies were bound from cradle to grave. On that day, I could hear, I can almost imagine that sound, that piercing sound of an ambulance that joggles your mind. Our caretaker

Dad at Marilyn's crypt in 1982

and friend, Earl, had phoned me in L.A.: "Your father has been rushed to the hospital. They don't know if he'll make it." I couldn't cry, I couldn't feel, all I could think was to hope and pray we would make it there in time. The thought of Dad's determination was cemented in my heart and brain. I repeatedly assured myself that he was a survivor to the core. He had survived the orphanages, the Gestapo hit list, the demise of Hollywood's studio system, and in the last four years, three cancer operations. A man who had taught me that life was worth living and we have a responsibility to stand up and be counted was going to survive tonight and not open the door to death's fatal knock.

My son Josh and I had arrived safely from L.A. at the Desert Hospital's emergency entrance in less than an hour and twenty minutes. A miracle in itself.

Running in, I caught his good friend, Dr. De Crinis's eye, searching, trying to decipher his expression before he spoke. He said, "Susan, your dad made it—a miracle."

In reality, Dad had attempted suicide.

Thus, began my search and understanding of the osmosis between two artists, my father and Norma Jean. Dad carefully orchestrating his final intentions in a state of unresolved torment and depression—not coincidentally, in the same way his beloved Marilyn had decades earlier. According to his own words, "Her death on this particular date was accidental rather than intentional. When through some unfortunate communication gaps in her last frantic calls for help no rescue came in time, she anesthetized her torment with more of the lethal mixture: drugs and alcohol."

Time ran out. Two orphans were running against time, forever fearful that their tragic pasts would grab them by the throat and hang them from the fragile tree they were born under. Their constant inferiority complexes allowed no defeats, so they were obsessed and ultimately possessed that they would have to become bigger than life in order to survive. Anything less was meaningless. Dad was the first to admit he was having a fifty-year love affair with the camera. It was the heartbeat of his existence and a perpetual obsession that gave him great satisfaction and sorrowful regret. When cancer began to stifle his art, his life became meaningless and he wrote:

> Dear Susan, and Josh,
>   Much as I've tried, I can't go on like this. After five operations in three years, I see the hopelessness of fighting this insidious sickness. I can feel that my body has lost its strength and my spirit refuses to see me disintegrate from a dynamic human being to a helpless invalid. . . .

Norma Jean and Dad both had a recurring longing for creative deaths; their attempted suicides can almost be viewed as symbolic sacrifices for one's art. For Norma,

In Bernard's own hand.

It was on a Saturday 20 years ago that a deeply depressed, lonely young woman left silently the noisy revolving stage called life.

she could not bear life knowing her aspirations for artistic acceptance as a serious actress would never be achieved. Her atonement for her part in the pact of letting the soul of the innately decent Norma Jean be transformed into the ultimate love goddess left her in a state of permanent insecurity: "As a person, my work is important to me. My work is the only ground I've ever had to stand on. Acting is very important. To put it bluntly, I seem to have a whole superstructure with no foundation. But I am working on the foundation."

In Marilyn's unfinished memoirs, she quoted Goethe: "Talent can be developed only in private. . . ." a status that, according to her, she never enjoyed. Sophia Loren had a full empathetic understanding when she observed in her autobiography, "I wept when I heard Marilyn Monroe was dead. . . . Only Marilyn knew why she died, which of her torments goaded her to death." In her meaninglessness and despair Marilyn overlooked the second half of Goethe's saying: ". . . and character is formed in the maelstrom of the world." Therein lies Marilyn's ultimate failure—her detachment from reality, her inability to keep her private life and professional life sufficiently apart.

Maybe her state of frustration was clearly mirrored in one of her last poems:

> *Help help*
> *Help I feel life coming closer*
> *When all I want is to die.*

Did Dad and she both live on the edge of hell towards their end? Had Marilyn become a victim of schizophrenia, a disease that has proven to be genetic in the 1990s? Dad's personality began disintegrating in the form of being humiliated and dehumanized when cancer, wearing the black boot of Hitler, began convincing him that a mysterious someone was taking his possessions and him violently away.

In the thick stack of Dad's unfinished memoirs, I discovered my theory on the parallels in their lives was sadly justified.

> . . . A new name and a new life could not uproot the cultural past which continued to govern the subsequent stages of my turbulent life. The connecting link between my experience in the Old and New Worlds is the dehumanization of man. As a survivor of the spiritual holocaust, I cannot transmit to anyone who never experienced it the shame, and humiliation to which we were exposed, officially categorized as "vermin" who could and should be treated as such. In my "second life" in the United States I could observe another dehumanization process which by elevating certain show business Personalities to the unreal status of gods and goddesses wrought irreparable harm on the psyche of those idols.

Dad's quest for artistic perfection stretched over half a century. His search for greatness of spirit compelled him to be a compulsive perfectionist, prompting him to strive to unveil the mirrored essence of Norma Jean/Marilyn, which was unattainable. His search brought him great joy when, sometimes, he was close to his ideal of the child-woman and above all the embodiment of joie de vivre and eternal femininity. It kept him young, forever adventurous and always seeking another triumph, aware that his heart, his intellect and strength of mind and spirit were the lenses of his cameras.

> *"The truly creative artist lives only after his death."*
>
> —CURT GOETZ